EYE TO EYE
with Cats

Maine Coon Cats

Lynn M. Stone

ROURKE PUBLISHING
Vero Beach, Florida 32964

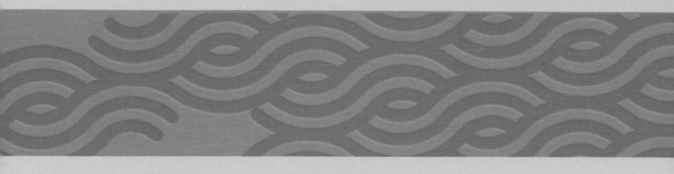

www.rourkepublishing.com

PHOTO CREDITS: © Kirill Vorobyev: 5, 10; © Butinova Elena: 8, 20, 22; © Nancy Nehring: 9; © Karen Town: 15; © Dave Raboin: 16, 17; © Lynn M. Stone: all other photos

Editor: Jeane Sturm

Cover and Page Design by Heather Botto

Library of Congress Cataloging-in-Publication Data

Stone, Lynn M.
 Maine coon cats / Lynn M. Stone.
    p. cm. -- (Eye to eye with cats)
 Includes index.
 ISBN 978-1-60694-337-3 (hard cover)
 ISBN 978-1-60694-863-7 (soft cover)
 1. Maine coon cat--Juvenile literature. I. Title.
 SF449.M34 S76 2010
 636.8/3--dc22
                                    2009005986

Printed in the USA

CG/CG

ROURKE PUBLISHING

www.rourkepublishing.com - rourke@rourkepublishing.com
Post Office Box 643328 Vero Beach, Florida 32964

Table of Contents

The Maine Coon is a large, handsome cat with long, silky fur. Despite its name, the Maine Coon is all cat and all American.

This **breed**, or kind, probably earned its name because, like a raccoon, it has a bushy, **ringed** tail and loves to climb trees.

The Maine Coon's big, round feet help it make its way through winter snow.

Modern day Maine Coons do not always have ringed tails. But the cats come in a wide range of more than 60 color patterns, many of them striped.

Maine Coons sport coats of many different colors, including this tabby and white combination.

If you want a smart kitty, a Maine Coon cat is a good choice because they are known for their intelligence.

The Maine Coon is one of the biggest breeds, with males being much larger than females. The heavy, shiny coat and **tufted** ears make Maine Coons look even bigger.

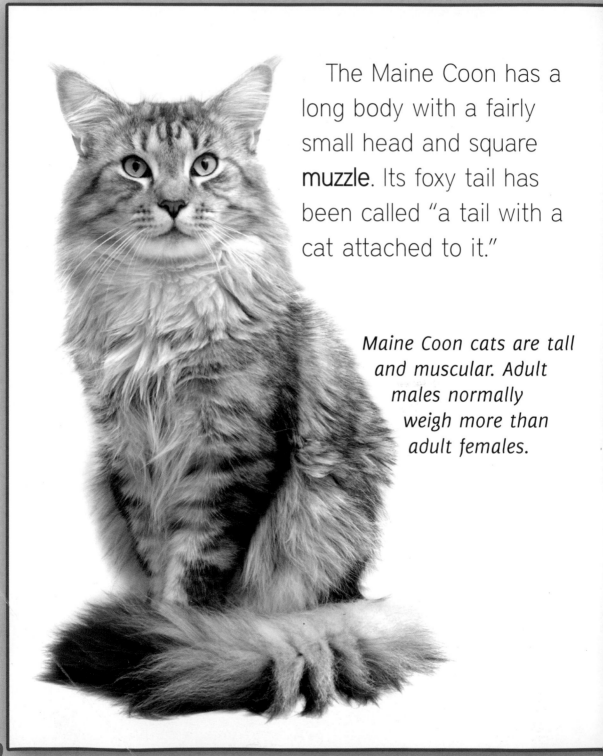

The Maine Coon has a long body with a fairly small head and square **muzzle**. Its foxy tail has been called "a tail with a cat attached to it."

Maine Coon cats are tall and muscular. Adult males normally weigh more than adult females.

Most Maine Coons have roundish eyes of green, green-gold, or gold. White Maine Coons may have blue eyes.

The Maine Coon's eyes are typically large and wide set.

A Maine Coon kitten whose parents are both Maine Coon cats is a **purebred**, like its parents. A purebred is simply a cat of pure breed.

Most cats are mixes of breeds. Cat **fanciers** like purebreds because they are predictable.

Many Maine Coons have white fur along their chins and lips.

Many purebred cat owners raise their cats to show. Judges grade cats based upon the ideal characteristics, or standards, of the breed. Cats were shown at fairs at least as far back as the 1860s. The first formal cat show was probably in 1871 in London, England. The most popular cat there was a Persian. The first major cat show in North America was held in 1895. The big winner there was a Maine Coon.

Maine Coons develop slowly, not reaching full size until they are 3-5 years old.

Kittens born to purebred parents typically grow up with the same type of fur and body type as their parents.

Someone who wanted Maine Coons with the broad face of the British look would choose that type of Maine Coon as parents.

Rather than a soft meow, Maine Coons communicate with their owners and other cats with a distinctive trill.

Maine Coon cats are good buddy cats. They are not usually lap cats. They like attention and return it, but they are fairly **independent**. Their greeting is often a cheery chirp rather than a meow.

Maine Coons are hardy cats, strong and heavily **furred**. They can be excellent hunters, and they do well outdoors. Like other purebreds, however, Maine Coons are generally kept indoors, out of harm's way.

Maine Coons have a loving and kind nature, and are good with families.

Maine Coons are playful and energetic without being house wreckers. They are also unusually **nimble** with their paws, although not quite in a raccoon's class. (Watch the water bowls!)

Male Maine Coons generally clown around a bit more than females.

The History of Maine Coons

The Maine Coon's heavy coat and tufted ears protect it from the snow and cold in harsher climates.

The actual **ancestors** of the Maine Coon cat can only be guessed. We do know that the breed came from the forest country of Maine.

It is likely that the breed's ancestors began to arrive on sailing ships in Maine's **seaports** some 300 years ago. Among those cats were probably longhairs from Russia and Scandinavia.

Maine Coons enjoy being around their owners. They will follow them from room to room, taking time to investigate their new surroundings.

Over time, these cats and their **offspring** grew increasingly common and alike. Farmers loved them for their hunting ability. By the 1860s, they were being shown at the Skowhegan Fair in Maine.

The arrival of Persian cats in America stole some of the Maine Coon's popularity in the early 20th century. Today, however, the Maine Coon is back as one of the most popular cats in North America and the world.

ABOUT CAT BREEDS

The beginnings of domestic, or tame, cats date back at least 8,000 years, when people began to raise the kittens of small wild cats. By 4,000 years ago, the Egyptians had totally tame, household cats. Most actual breeds of cats, however, are fewer than 150 years old. People created breeds by selecting parent cats that had certain qualities people liked and wanted to repeat. Two longhaired parents, for example, were likely to produce longhaired kittens. By carefully choosing cat parents, cat fanciers have managed to create cats with predictable qualities—breeds.

Maine Coon Facts

- 🐾 Date of Origin – 1800s

- 🐾 Place of Origin – New England, United States

- 🐾 Overall Size – large

- 🐾 Weight – 9-22 pounds (4-10 kilograms)

- 🐾 Coat – medium long, dense

- 🐾 **Grooming** – twice weekly

- 🐾 Activity Level – average

- 🐾 **Temperament** – fairly affectionate; needs attention

- 🐾 Voice – quiet

Glossary

ancestors (AN-sess-turz): those past members of a family, usually before one's grandparents

breed (BREED): a particular kind of domestic animal, such as a Maine Coon cat

fanciers (FAN-see-erz): those who raise and work to improve purebred cats

furred (FURD): to be covered by fur

grooming (GROOM-ing): the act of brushing, combing, and cleaning

independent (in-di-PEN-duhnt): free from the control of people or things

muzzle (MUHZ-uhl): an animal's nose, mouth, and jaws; its face

nimble (NIM-buhl): to move easily and lightly, especially with hands or paws

offspring (OF-spring): the young (babies) of an animal

purebred (PYOOR-bred): an animal with ancestors of the same breed

ringed (RINGD): to be marked by a pattern of circles, or rings

seaports (SEE-ports): cities or towns with harbors for ships

temperament (TEM-pur-uh-muhnt): an animal's nature or personality

tufted (TUHFT-ed): a small patch of hair that stands up and apart

Index

Websites to Visit

kids.cfa.org/

www.ticaeo.com

www.cfainc.org/breeds/profiles/maine.html

About the Author

A former teacher and sports writer, Lynn Stone is a widely published children's book author and nature photographer. He has photographed animals on all seven continents. The National Science Teachers Association chose one of his books, *Box Turtles*, as an Outstanding Science Trade Book for 2008. Stone, who grew up in Connecticut, lives in northern Illinois with his wife, golden retriever, two cats, and abundant fishing tackle.